I0759458

This book
belongs to

make believe ideas ltd

The Wilderness, Berkhamsted, Hertfordshire, HP4 2AZ, UK.
557 Broadway, New York, NY 10012, USA.

Manufactured in China.

www.makebelieveideas.com

With illustrations by Danielle Mudd.

101 5-minute devotions

With illustrations by Danielle Mudd

make believe ideas

Contents

For a **themed contents list**, please see the back of the book.

"Hello, God!"

What a big yawn! Do you yawn and stretch when you wake up? What else do you do? Lucas likes to say hello to God at the start of the day. Some mornings he talks to him about what he has planned to do. But sometimes he just says, "What shall we do today, God?"

King David talked to God in the morning. Read Psalm 5:3.

"God, it's great that I can talk to you any time of the day. Thank you for listening to me. Amen."

A sunny day

Have you heard how much noise the birds make when the sun rises in the morning? Or maybe you've seen the beautiful sky when the sun sets in the evening. God made it all, and he wants us to praise him from first thing in the morning until we go to bed.

Psalm 113:3 tells us to praise God all day long.

**“Dear God,
I'll thank you in the morning,
I'll praise you all day long,
and in the evening, dear God,
I'll sing a thank-you song.
Amen.”**

3

Wonderful hair

God made us very carefully. We are different shapes and sizes. Even our hair is different. What color is your hair? Is it black or brown, red or blonde? Is it thick or thin, straight or curly? Is it long, short, or in-between?

Judges 13 tells the story of Samson-the-warrior's birth. His hair grew long to show that he belonged to God.

"Dear God, you created me from my toes to my hair! You gave me all I have, God. Thank you for your care! Amen."

Each of your hairs

Do you know how many hairs you have on your head? It would take a very long time to count them all. But Jesus said that God loves you so much and knows you so well that he knows exactly how many hairs you have. Isn't that amazing?

"You're great, God! You know everything about me and you love me. Thank you. Amen."

Jesus explained to his friends how much God cares for each of us. See Matthew 10:29–31.

Feeling happy

How can you tell that these children are happy? Some people hum, whistle, or sing when they're happy. When something really good happens, they might skip, dance, or shout to show how happy they are. What do you do when you're really happy?

God likes it when we shout for joy! Read Psalm 68:3.

**"Dear God,
I jump and dance
to show you
how glad I am
to know you!
Amen."**

Singing

What's your favorite song? Do you know any songs about God? God loves to hear us sing to him. It doesn't matter if you can't sing in tune or if you forget the words. God loves to hear you. If you sing with others, it can make a fantastic sound!

**"Dear God,
I want to sing; I want to shout and praise you!
Amen."**

Psalm 66:1–4 tells us to sing and shout praises to God!

7

Going to school

Zac likes going to school. He likes meeting up with his friend Hasan. How do you get to school? Do you walk, or do you go by car or bus? Next time you're going somewhere, remember to thank God. Thank him for your car or for the bus, or thank him that you can walk.

Jesus sent his friends out on a long walk. See Luke 10:1–9.

“Dear God, thank you for buses and thank you for trains. Thank you that cars keep us dry when it rains. Amen.”

Friends

When you're hurt or feeling ill, friends help you and care for you. A friend will hold your hand, pat your arm, or give you a hug. A friend will sit quietly with you when you don't want to run around and play. A friend understands when you're sad. Let's thank God for giving us friends!

"Thanks, God, for giving me friends who care for me. Help me to be a caring friend to them too. Amen."

The people in Acts 9:36–41 ask Peter to come to help their friend.

9

Cuts and bruises

Olivia was going fast on her scooter, then she fell off. Her knee started bleeding. Olivia's knee feels really sore today. But do you know what's amazing? In a week or so, it will be almost healed! God has given us bodies that do really awesome things.

"Ouch! It really hurt when I fell! Dear God, please make me well. Amen."

People who care

God makes sure there are lots of people to take care of us. There are people to care for us at home and at day care or school. Can you think of someone who takes care of you? What kind of people do caring jobs?

Joseph isn't Jesus' father, but he takes very good care of him. Read Matthew 1:18–25.

"Thank you, God, for all the people who take care of me. I want to give thanks especially for .... Amen."

Enjoy your books

Reading books is fun! You can read exciting stories. You can find out what happened long ago. You can discover wonderful things about the world God has made, from planets to plants and rockets to rainbows. And when you read God's special book, the Bible, you learn about God.

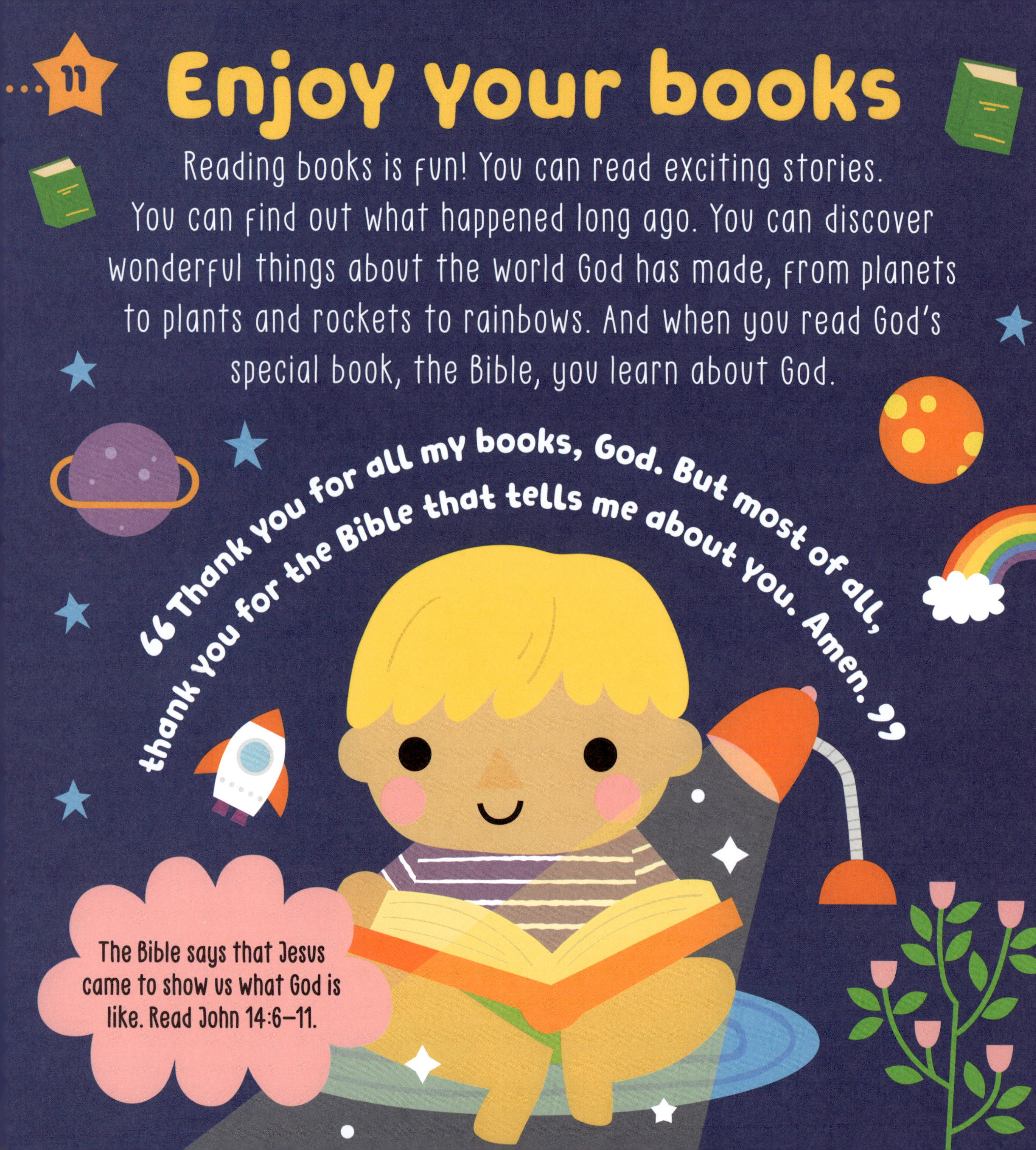

Grow and Learn

Growing up is fun because we learn to do new things. What can you do now that you couldn't do when you were little? Can you ride a bike, catch a ball, or read a book? God wants us to become more like Jesus as we grow up. Jesus loved God and was kind and good to others.

Jesus asked his friends to love one another. Read John 15:12–14.

“Help me, Jesus, to grow more like you – loving God and others too. Amen.”

13
Sharing
Have you ever had friends over to play at your house? Or maybe you've had people who have come for dinner or to stay overnight. It's exciting having visitors! It's fun to share our toys, food, and homes with others. It makes God happy too because he shares everything he has made with us!
“Dear God, help me to be like you and share my home and my toys with others. Amen.”
How does God feel when we share what we have with others? Read Hebrews 13:16.

Caring and giving

God wants us to be caring, giving people. We can give food and clothes to others who need them. The clothes that are too small for you might fit your younger brother or sister. And if your brother or sister doesn't need them, you can give them away to someone who does!

When we help others, we show Jesus that we love him. Read Matthew 25:31–40.

Donations

SHAPES

"Dear God, please take care of people who are in need. Show me how I can help them. Amen."

Your brain

God has given you a brain, and it's very important. It tells your body what to do so you can move, eat, and brush your teeth. It helps you figure out what to say before you say it. You use it to remember what you've done today and to think about what you want to do tomorrow. Isn't that amazing?

**“Dear God,
thank you for my brain.
Help me to use it well.
Amen.”**

Other people may not know what you're thinking, but God does! See Psalm 139:1–2.

Let's pretend

God has given us sharp minds so that we can imagine. Leo is really good at imagining. He loves playing make-believe games. He pretends he's a brave knight. He likes playing the hero and rescuing his friends. Do you play games like that? Who do you like to be?

"I'm glad I can imagine, God. When I play make believe, I like to be

....

Amen."

David is a real hero. He isn't big or strong, but he knows God will help him win. Read 1 Samuel 17:32–50.

Feeling sad

Sometimes things happen that make us very, very sad. When someone we love a lot goes away or when our pet dies, we can feel sad, angry, and empty inside. Jesus understands how we feel. When sad things happen to you, Jesus will be there to love you and help you. You can talk to him.

Jesus was very sad when his friend Lazarus died. Find out more in John 11:1–3, 17, 32–35.

“Jesus, I know that you love me. I know that you listen. I want to tell you that I feel very sad about .... Amen.”

Talking to God

Prayer is talking to God. It doesn't matter whether we talk to God with our eyes open or closed. It doesn't matter if we're standing up, sitting down, lying in our beds, or kneeling. We can talk to God anywhere and everywhere. We can talk to him out loud or in our heads.

"Dear God, I know I can talk to you about anything. I want to tell you about .... Amen."

Jesus taught his friends a special prayer. You can find it in Matthew 6:9–13.

19 Lots of Languages

Isn't God awesome? He made us all so different. We look different and sound different. We even speak to him in different languages. These friends are saying hello in their own languages. Can you figure out who speaks French, who speaks Spanish, who speaks Hindi, and who speaks English?

“Dear God, it's amazing that we can talk to you in so many different ways. It's wonderful that you understand us and love us all. Thank you. Amen.”

Caring for Earth

God made so many different people. He made men, women, boys, and girls, and he put us in different places and different countries. But God has given us all the important job of taking care of the world. There are lots of ways we can do that. Can you think of some?

“Dear God, you made us all. Help us take care of one another. Help us all to care for your world. Amen.”

It was God's idea to give us the job of caring for his world. Read Genesis 1:26–31.

The doctor

Sometimes when we're ill, we need to see a doctor. God has given doctors the important job of figuring out what is wrong with our bodies. Doctors spend a long time learning about how God has made us. They know which medicines will help us to get better quickly.

Jesus was the best doctor of all. He made people better without any medicine. Read Matthew 4:23–24.

“Lord God, thank you for giving us doctors to care for us when we're ill. Amen.”

Worrying

Did you know that God loves you so much he wants to help you when you're worried? You may worry about starting school or going to a new playgroup. You might worry when it gets dark or when you have to walk past a barking dog. Talk to God about the things that worry you.

When you get worried, remember what Peter wrote to his friends. Read 1 Peter 5:7.

"Hello God, I get worried about .... When I feel like that, please help me. Amen."

"I'm sorry!"

What happens when you argue or fight with your brother or sister? Do your mom and dad sort things out? Or do you say "I'm sorry" and make friends again? Jesus tells us that saying sorry and forgiving each other is the best way. It's hard to do, but Jesus will help you.

There's a story in Genesis 50:15–21 about Joseph's brothers saying sorry for being mean to him.

"Sometimes we fight, and we know it's not right. Help us to say sorry. Help us to love, just like you, our father above. Amen."

"It's okay."

How do you feel when a friend says they're sorry for hurting you or breaking your toy? Yasmin feels a little better now that Zara has said she's sorry, but she still feels a bit angry. Yasmin knows that when someone says they're sorry, she should try to forgive them so they can be friends again.

"Dear God, help me to forgive other people like you forgive me. Amen."

Ears

Close your eyes and listen carefully. What different sounds can you hear? God gave us ears so that we can hear loud noises and quiet sounds. We need ears to listen to music and to one another. Isn't it great that God created ears?

"Thank you, God, for my two ears. Thank you, God, that I can hear. Amen."

Find out what happens to a man who cannot hear or talk in Mark 7:31–37.

Praise

From Alaska to Australia, from Chile to China, from Nigeria to Norway, men and women, boys and girls sing songs of praise to God, who made us all. The whole world and everyone in it belong to him. He loves and cares for us all. What a wonderful God!

“Dear God, it's amazing that you love and care for everybody in the world. I'm glad I belong to you. You're great, God! Amen.”

Psalm 86:8–10 is a song about how powerful and wonderful God is. There is no one like him!

27

Where do You Live?

Can you find where you live on a map or a globe?
God made every country in the world. He made some with high mountains and some with green hills or deep canyons. Others have long beaches or rocky shores.

Psalm 95:3–5 is a song about God's world. Why not make up a tune for it?

Wet and wonderful

It roars, waves, and crashes. It's salty, wet, and huge! It covers most of Earth. Can you guess what it is? Yes – the ocean! It's amazingly deep and full of all kinds of weird and wonderful creatures. And God made it all.

Read about God making the oceans in Genesis 1:1–10.

"You make the oceans swirl and roar, you make the waves crash on the shore. You are awesome. You are great. Thank you, God, for all you make! Amen."

A baby sister

At first Toby was pleased that God had given him a new sister. But when baby Chloe came home from the hospital, Toby got annoyed because Mom was always busy with Chloe. Sharing your mom and dad with someone else can be hard. God knows how you feel. You can talk to him and he always listens.

"Dear God, help my friend .... to love their new sibling. Amen."

Exodus 2:1–10 is the story of a big sister who takes care of her baby brother.

How many people are in your family? Do you know how many people there are in God's family? Too many to count! God's family is made up of all the people who love him and know that God loves them too. In God's family, we can sing and dance, and we can find out how much he loves us!

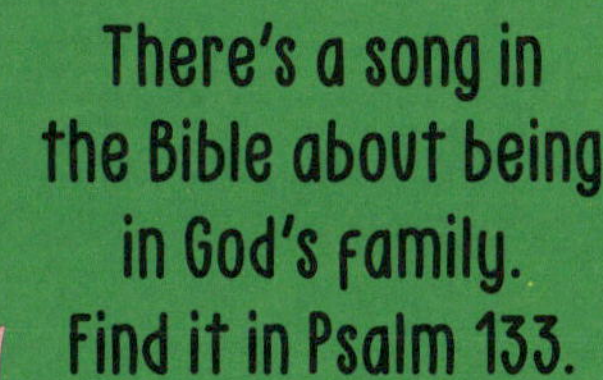

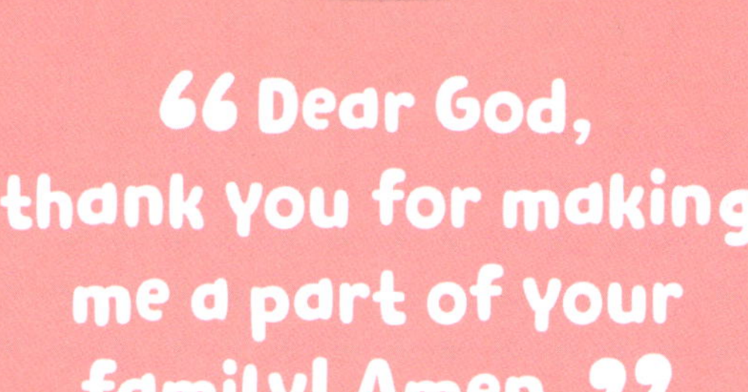

Making faces

Rory and Kai are practicing funny faces! Making faces can be fun, but if you're doing it to be rude, then that's not kind. Sometimes Rory and his friends call one another names too. They do it for fun, but it's easy to hurt someone's feelings. What do you think God would want them to do?

Read Ephesians 4:29 to find out how God wants us to speak to one another.

"Dear God, when my friends and I are having fun, help us to speak kindly to one another. Amen."

Feeling angry

Sometimes our friends upset us when they say unkind things or won't let us play with them. When we're upset, we may get angry and say something unkind back. Jesus said that when someone does something mean to us, we must not be mean to them. Instead, Jesus wants us to be kind to them.

33

Happy birthday

When is your birthday? How old will you be?
On your birthday, your family celebrates the day you were born.
Sometimes they might give you a present to make you feel special.
Perhaps they also thank God for giving them such a precious child.

Psalm 127:3 reminds us that each new person is a special gift from God.

**“Dear God, thank you for loving me.
Thank you for my family that loves me too. Amen.”**

“Thank you!”

A present! How exciting! Hopefully Jessica remembers to say thank you. The Bible tells us to keep on thanking God for all that he gives us. You can thank God in your prayers. What do you want to thank God for?

“Thank you, God, for all your good gifts. Today I give thanks for

....

Amen.”

Psalm 136 is a song of thanks. Use verses 1–9 and 23–26 to help you with your prayer.

Being sick

It's miserable being sick. When you have a sore tummy or you've hurt yourself, what makes you feel better? Medicines, bandages, and lotions help our bodies to heal. Cuddles from our loved ones help us to feel better too!

Discover how a very sick, unhappy woman gets better in Mark 5:25–34.

"Dear God, I know you care for me when I'm not well. Thank you for .... that makes me feel much better. Amen."

Cuddles

Ida loves cuddling her mom. Who gives you a hug? Ida's mom cuddles her when she's sad. She cuddles her at bedtime and hugs her just to say how much she loves her. Ida is very glad that God has given her a mom to love and take care of her.

"I like it when I'm cuddled. Thank you, God, for my family. Amen."

Read Mark 7:24–30 and find out how Jesus helps a mom.

Amazing eyes

Look around you. What can you see? Can you see something blue? Can you see something round? God has made a world with all sorts of colors and shapes. And he has given us eyes to see it all. Isn't God great?

Jesus helped two men to see again. Read Matthew 20:29–34.

"Thank you, God, for eyes to see. Thank you, God, for making me! Amen."

Wonderful flowers

God made flowers beautiful. They each have their own special shape and smell. He made flowers that climb walls, ones that grow close to the ground, and others that stand up tall. If God cares about flowers, we can be sure he cares for us too.

“Dear God, it’s wonderful that you care about the tiniest flower. And even though I’m little, I know you care for me too. Amen.”

Jesus told us that God cares about all the little things. Read Luke 12:27–28.

Toys

God has given us a wonderful world to live in. We have great toys to play with. What is your favorite toy? Josie loves playing on her roller skates. Some toys are fun to play with on your own, and others are great to play with friends.

“God, sometimes when I go out, I ride, hide, climb, and shout. I like to bounce, and I love to run. Thank you for friends to share the fun! Amen.”

The Bible reminds us to thank God for all he gives us. See Psalm 104:33–34.

Being friendly

We know that pinching or kicking is unfriendly. But we're also being unfriendly when we tease people or don't let them join in. Jesus wants us to be kind to everyone. If you see someone being teased or left out, what can you do to be friendly?

"Dear Jesus, I'm sorry that at times I've been unfriendly. Help me speak kindly and invite others to play. Amen."

Find out who is friendly to Paul when he is left out. Read Acts 9:26–28.

Feeling scared

Alicia likes going to school now, but she was very scared on her first day. Have you ever been scared of going somewhere new? When we're afraid, we can talk to God. He is bigger and more powerful than everything – even the things we're scared of!

Make up a tune for the words from Psalm 56:3 so you can remember them when you're scared.

"Dear God, when I'm scared, help me remember that you love me and that you will help me. Amen."

Your best friend

Did you know that God is your best friend? You can tell him anything! Whether you're sad, happy, angry, or scared, God will always listen to you. He'll never leave you or say he doesn't want to be your friend. He's always by your side.

David loved being a friend of God. Look how he describes his friend, God, in 2 Samuel 22:1–4.

“God, I love you. Thank you for being such a great friend. Amen.”

43 Animals galore

How many different animals can you think of? God made all sorts of animals. He made tall ones and tiny ones, smooth ones and wrinkly ones, scaly ones and furry ones. God has thought of everything!

“You’re great, God! I’m glad you made so many different animals. The animal I like best is .... Amen.”

Read Genesis 1:20–25 to find out how God feels about the animals he made.

Caring for plants

God filled his world with all kinds of plants, and he wants us to take care of them. We can do that by planting seeds or watering a house plant. When we're outside, we can enjoy wildflowers by looking at them instead of picking them.

Putting toys away

Jackie loves playing with the big jigsaw puzzles at preschool. But now she has to put them away. She wants to keep playing, but she knows that everything must be cleaned up before story time. What things do you put away?

“I've played with all my toys, God; they're scattered on the floor. Now it's time to clean up. Tomorrow I'll play some more! Amen.”

Read John 6:5–13 to find out what Jesus' friends have to clean up.

Together

It's fun playing with friends! Have you noticed that when you do a jigsaw puzzle with your friends, you finish it faster? It's the same when it's time to clean up. When everyone helps and works together, it doesn't take long to get the job done.

Paul is glad to have lots of friends to work with. How many are mentioned in Colossians 4:7–14?

"Together we talk and put away; together we work and play. Together we live to love you, God. Help us love one another today. Amen."

Resting

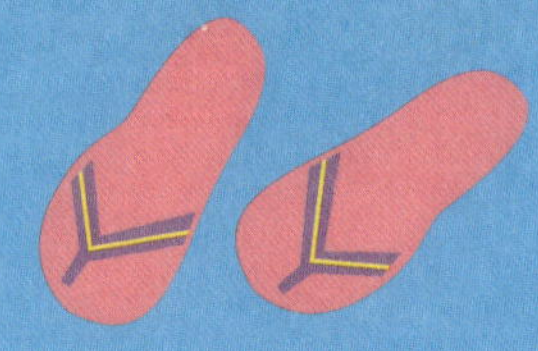

Did you know that holidays are God's idea? When God finished making the world, he gave everyone a holiday. He made a special day each week when we don't have to go to school – we can enjoy being with him. We can rest and enjoy everything God has given us. What do you do on Sunday?

"Thank you, God, that we have days to rest. What a great idea! I like to .... to relax. Amen."

Read about God giving everyone a day of rest in Genesis 2:1–3.

“Let me shout!”

When we feel really excited, we can't keep it inside. We get a bubbly, happy, fizzy feeling that makes us want to jump, run, or dance around. When we're excited, it's hard to keep quiet, isn't it? We can't help shouting or cheering. What do you do when you're excited?

“Hello, God. I get really excited when

....

It makes me want to

....

Amen.”

A book of stories

The Bible is full of exciting stories, such as the story of how God made the world. There are also sad stories, such as the story of Adam and Eve disobeying God. But the most wonderful story is about Jesus, who came to make us friends with God again.

"Thank you, God, for the Bible. Thank you for

....

who tells me the stories of Jesus. Amen."

Listening to God

God made us, loves us, and cares for us. He is our dad in heaven. God loves it when we talk to him. He wants us to listen to him too. That's why he has given us the Bible: so that we can find out what he wants to say to us.

Jesus came from heaven to show us what our father God is like. Read John 6:44–47.

“Dear Father in heaven, I'm glad I can talk to you. Please help me to hear what you are saying to me. Amen.”

51 Loving our siblings

It's great having a brother or sister! But sometimes we make each other angry, then we say and do things that aren't loving at all. Jesus wants us to love one another, even when we're annoyed. It's hard, but he can help us not to shout, be rude, or be mean.

"Dear Lord Jesus, I need your help to be kind and loving when my siblings make me angry. Amen."

When Martha gets upset with her sister, she tells Jesus how she feels. See Luke 10:38–42.

Helping others

Jesus wants us to be helpful. There are lots of ways we can help at home and at school. Claire is helping her baby sister practice walking. You might help someone at school put on their shoes or button their coat. How else could you help your brother, sister, or friends?

Jesus tells a story about a man who helps someone in Luke 10:25–37.

"Jesus, you are always helping others. I want to be helpful just like you. Amen."

Can you smell it?

God gave you your nose. He made it especially for smelling. Your nose can tell you if something is good to eat or not. It can smell smoke to warn you of dangerous fires. We love some smells and hate others! What smell do you like most?

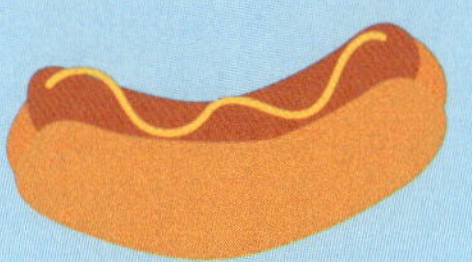

Tasty food

Dad cooked the meal, but where did the food come from? The supermarket, of course! But before that? From a farm or a factory! But before that? From God! He has made so many things that we can eat and enjoy. What's your favorite food?

"Tomatoes, beans, spaghetti, or meat – thank you, God, for the food I eat! Amen."

Read about a wonderful picnic in Matthew 15:32–38, and see how Jesus thanks God for food.

Planting a tree

God made lots of different plants and trees. If you want to grow a tree, you need a seed. If you plant a seed and give it water and light, it will grow. It takes years for trees to grow, so you'll have to be very patient!

"Thank you, God,
for the trees so tall.
It's awesome they start as
seeds so small! Amen."

What seed does Jesus talk about? Find out in Mark 4:30–32.

A windy day

God makes the wind. He makes the gentle breeze that cools your face and the howling gale that can blow down a tree. You can't see the wind, but you can see what the wind does, and you can feel it. How do you know if it's a windy day?

God sent a strong wind to help Moses and the Israelites. Read Exodus 14:10–22.

“Thank you for the wind that cools the hottest summer day, and brings the clouds to give us rain, then blows them all away! Amen.”

Lonely

Ronen is feeling lonely. No one wants to play with him. If you ever feel like Ronen, just remember that God always wants to be your friend. He never leaves you on your own. Even though you can't see him, he is there. He loves you.

No one wanted to be friends with Zacchaeus. Find out what happened when he met Jesus in Luke 19:1–10.

“When no one wants to be with me and no one seems to care, I know that you're my friend, dear God. I know you're always there. Amen.”

God cares

God cares when you feel alone. He cares when your hamster dies. He cares when you fall off the swing. And he knows how you feel when you miss someone. No matter what happens, God cares for you.

Poor Joseph was put in prison! But even in prison, God took care of him. Read Genesis 39:19–23.

"Dear God, I know you care for me. Today I feel sad about .... Amen."

Arguing

We all argue and fight sometimes, even with our friends. Can you think of things you argue or fight about? Maybe you and your friend sometimes fight over toys or argue about whose turn it is. Jesus knows we argue and fight, and that's why he tells us to love one another, say we're sorry, and forgive.

What did Jesus say when his friends were arguing? See Luke 22:24–27.

“Jesus, when I start to argue and fight with my friends, help me to stop and say sorry. Amen.”

Taking turns

"I want to go first!" If everybody said that, there would be a big argument! There are some games that don't work very well if we all try to play at the same time. Can you think of games where you have to take turns? Next time you play, practice letting your friend go first!

"Lord Jesus, it's hard to let others go first. Please help me to wait my turn and say, 'You go first!' Amen."

Abraham let his nephew, Lot, go first. Read Genesis 13:5–12.

61

A mouth for eating

We use our mouths to sing and talk, but what else do we use them for? Eating, of course! God gave us teeth to chew our food and a tongue to taste different flavors. There are lots of different types of food to try! What's your favorite flavor?

"God, you are great! You made all of me. Thank you for my mouth, my teeth, and my tongue. Amen."

Read 1 Kings 17:2–6 to discover who brings food for Elijah.

Parties

Do you like parties? They're so much fun! Make sure you don't leave anyone out. God gives us friends to share our special days with. Who will you invite to your next party? Ask God to help you make everyone feel really welcome.

Jesus eats with people who are often left out. Read Mark 2:15–17.

“Balloons and cake for everyone. Thank you, God, for party fun! Amen.”

Show your Love

How does your mom show you she loves you? Maybe she cooks for you, reads you stories, cleans your clothes, gives you hugs and kisses, tucks you into bed at night, and takes care of you when you're hurt or sick. How do you show your mom you love her?

Jesus didn't want his mother to be alone after he died, so he asked John to take care of her. Read John 19:25–27.

“Thank you for my family, God. Help me to show them I love them. Amen.”

Setting the table

God wants us to help one another. We can help our friends, our brothers and sisters, and even our moms and dads. Can you see how Ali is helping his mom? There are lots of other ways we can help at home. Can you think of some?

"Dear God, I help my parents when I

....

Amen."

Find out about the meal Jesus had with his friends. Read Luke 22:7–13.

Drawing

If you want to draw well, you have to keep on trying. Don't give up, and if it doesn't go well, try again! We often have to try hard to get things right. God can help us keep going and not give up. What's your favorite thing to draw?

The Bible encourages us not to give up following Jesus. See Hebrews 12:1–3.

"Dear God, I find

....

difficult to do. Help me to keep on trying and not give up. Amen."

A rainbow

Have you ever seen a rainbow? Jenna is painting one! She's heard the story of how God rescued Noah and the animals from a flood. God put a rainbow in the sky as a promise that he would never flood the Earth again. God keeps his promises!

"Dear God, thank you for keeping your promises. I know I can always trust you. Amen."

Read the amazing story of Noah and the ark in Genesis 7:1–9:17.

Guilty

Quite often we know we've done something naughty even before our parents scold us. We know we've done wrong because we feel bad inside. We feel guilty. When we feel like this, God wants us to say sorry. He always forgives us. He will help us make things right again.

“Dear God, when I know I've done something wrong, help me to say sorry and make things right. Amen.”

Psalm 51 is a song about saying sorry.

Obeying

Do you do what your mom asks? Sometimes Ava does what her mom asks right away, but other times she doesn't do what she's told at all! She doesn't mind vacuuming, but she hates putting her toys away. God wants Ava to listen to her mom and do what she says. He wants you to do that too!

Do you know what makes God happy? Find out in Colossians 3:20.

“Dear God, sometimes I find it hard to do what my parents say. Will you help me? Amen.”

Exciting stories

What kind of stories do you like? Do you like exciting adventures or books with pictures? Jesus told all kinds of stories. He wanted people to know how much God loved them. Crowds of people sat down and listened to Jesus. He was a great storyteller.

Read one of Jesus' stories. See Matthew 25:14–30.

“Dear God, thank you for stories that help me learn something new. Amen.”

Loving our dads

We show our dads we love them in lots of ways – when we paint them a picture, give them a hug, or do what they tell us to do. God is our dad too. He is our father in heaven. We can show him we love him by doing what he says.

"Father in heaven, I love you. Please help me to do what You say. Amen."

How can we show God that we love him? Find out in 1 John 5:2–3.

Tall Toby

Do you think Toby will be as tall as his big brother when he's older? Toby and Charlie don't know how tall they'll be when they grow up or whether they'll live to be 100 years old. But God knows all about Toby and Charlie, and you and me!

"Dear God, it's fun getting bigger and growing older. I'm going to be .... on my next birthday! Amen."

Caring for others

The world is full of different people. We look different and we live in different places, but God made us all. He wants us to love and help one another. When we care for one another, no one is left out or lonely.

“Thank you, God, for everyone. Help me to care for others the way You care for me. Amen.”

God didn't want Adam to be on his own, so he made a friend for him. Read Genesis 2:18–23.

Playing together

Playing is so much more fun with friends. Which friends do you like to play with? Sometimes Max, Aisha, and Grace play with Max's bricks, but today they're playing with Grace's train set. God is glad when we share and play kindly with our friends.

If you want to find out how God wants you to play with your friends, read 1 Thessalonians 5:15.

"Dear God, thank you for my friends. Please help us to play well together. Amen."

A broken toy

Have you ever had a really special toy that got broken? How did you feel? Could it be fixed? Isn't it a great feeling when something is mended again? God knows exactly how you feel when you're upset. And he is happy for you when things are fixed!

“Dear God, I'm really happy when things can be fixed. Thank you! Amen.”

Nehemiah rebuilds the broken walls of the city. How do the people thank God in Nehemiah 12:43?

Hands

Think of all the things you do with your hands. You use them to hold a fork, lift a bag, build a tower, or throw a ball. You use your hands to pat a dog, stroke a cat, blow a kiss, and wave hello. But when you pinch, shove, and hit, you are using your hands to hurt others. God wants our hands to help, not hurt.

Jesus uses his hands to help and love. Find out how in Mark 1:40–42.

"God, You gave me hands to help and love. Please help me not to pinch and shove. Amen."

Caring for animals

God told us to take care of his animals. If you had a pet rabbit, dog, or hamster, how would you keep it safe from danger? Did you know that leaving trash on the ground can be dangerous for wild animals and birds? When we put cans and plastic wrappers in the recycling or trash, we're helping to keep God's wild animals safe.

"Dear Lord God, I want to take care of your animals. Show me how I can keep them safe. Amen."

Jesus talks about himself as the Good Shepherd who cares for his sheep. Read John 10:11–16.

Sister Love

Do you have a sister? Ciara loves her big sister, Anna. She draws pictures for her and gives her big hugs. Anna loves Ciara too. She reads to her and plays with her. When they argue, they make up quickly. How do you show your sister you love her?

God said that if we love him, we must love our brothers and sisters too! See 1 John 4:21.

I you x

“Thank you, God, for my sister. Help me to show her that I love her even when she makes me angry. Amen.”

Being patient

We love our siblings, but sometimes they annoy us! God understands that we get mad. He wants us to learn to be kind, gentle, and patient. So the next time your brother or sister is annoying you, ask God to help you to be loving toward them.

**“Dear God,
You are kind and good. You are gentle and patient with me. Help me to be like you. Amen.”**

God helps us to grow more like him. See Galatians 5:22–23.

Cleaning

There are lots of ways we can help our parents. Can you think of some? Will helps with sweeping. He's very good with the dustpan and broom. He makes sure he gets all the dirt into the dustpan! How do you help at home?

"God, I can clean, I can sweep, and put my toys away. I can dust and polish too, helping every day. Amen."

Find out why a woman cleans her whole house in Luke 15:8–10.

What you do best

George is good at playing his toy saxophone, and Mia sings beautifully. Together they make a lovely sound! God made us all different. Some people are good at running, some are good at puzzles, and others are good at baking. What are you good at?

God uses people who are good at different things to help others.
See Acts 6:2–7.

“I'm glad you've made us all different, God. I'm good at .... and my friend is good at .... Amen.”

Feeling shy

Going to a new place or meeting new people can make us feel shy. When James feels shy, he doesn't want to talk; he wants to hide. He squeezes his favorite toy. God wants to help us when we feel like that. Although we can't see him, he is always with us.

If you feel shy, remember what the Bible says. See Proverbs 18:10.

"Dear God, when I feel shy, help me to remember that I'm safe with you. Amen."

Packing up

Hurry up, Stephen! The toys have to be packed away soon. It's moving day tomorrow! Stephen is excited about his new house, and he's a little nervous about making new friends. But he knows that God is always with him no matter where he lives.

In Matthew 2:13–14, God took care of Jesus' family when they moved to a new country.

"It's great to know that wherever I go, You are always with me. Thank you, God. Amen."

Legs

There are so many things we use our legs for – walking, running, hopping, jumping, cycling, swimming, and dancing. Try using your legs now! Can you balance on one leg? Can you hop like a frog? Can you point your toes? How about sitting cross-legged?

Find out who is walking and who is dancing in Exodus 15:19–20.

“I'm standing on one leg, Jesus. Now you see me hop! Look at me, I'm running. My legs never stop! Amen.”

Walking together

Sophie and Emily love walking to school together. They skip, run, and talk a lot! When Jesus and his friends walked together, Jesus would tell stories about the way God wanted them to live. Jesus is with you too, even as you go to school.

"Jesus, I want to walk with you.
Jesus, I want to talk with you.
Jesus, I want to be with you
the whole day through. Amen."

Grandparents

Our grandmas and grandpas are the moms and dads of our moms and dads. What do you call your grandparents? It doesn't matter whether they live just around the corner or far away, our grandmas and grandpas love and care for us.

“Thank you, God, for my grandparents. I love them because .... Amen.”

Naomi is very happy when her grandchild is born. See Ruth 4:13–16.

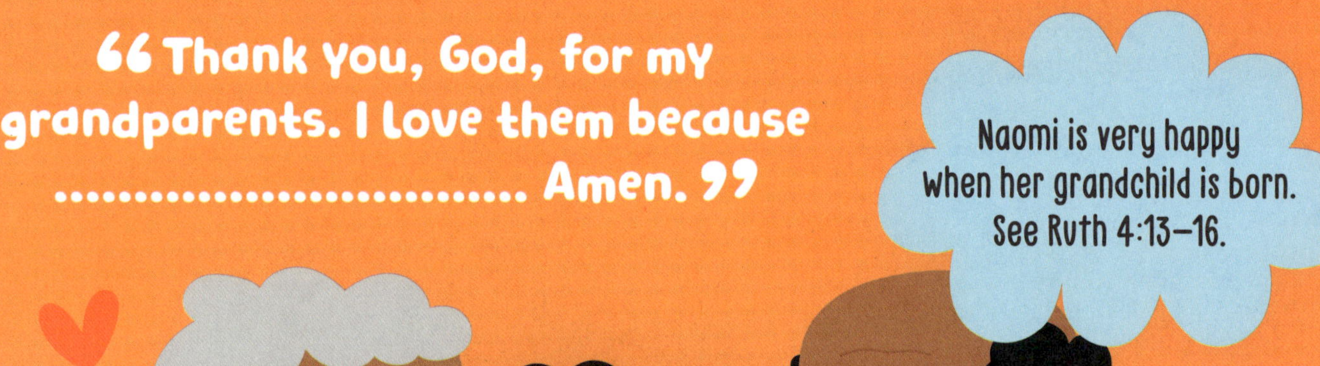

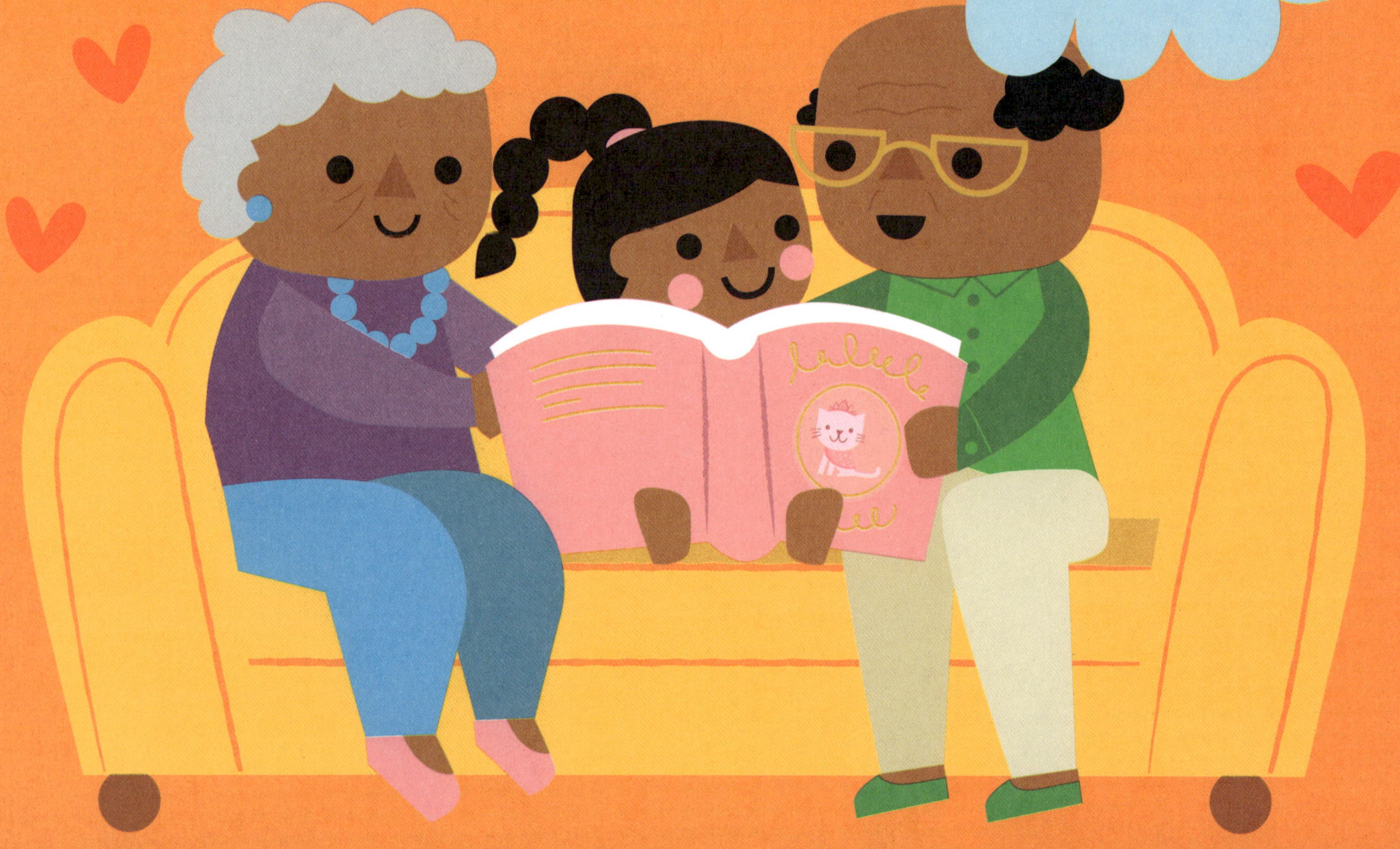

Keeping in touch

Nicola's aunt lives a long way away, so she doesn't see her very often. But they love to video call each other. We can't see God, but we can talk to him whenever we want by praying. We can talk to God out loud or in our heads. God loves to talk to us.

"I'm glad I can talk to you, dear God, anytime, night or day. Thanks for always listening when I stop to pray. Amen."

What are Samuel and God talking about in 1 Samuel 16:1–13?

87

Rain for the grass

Do you like rain? Or do you like sunshine every day? Imagine what would happen if it never rained! The grass wouldn't grow. The cows would have nothing to eat. They wouldn't make any milk, and we wouldn't have milkshakes, ice cream, or cheese for pizza! What a good thing God sends rain to make the grass grow!

Psalm 147:7–8 tells us that God sends the rain. What does it say we should do?

“Dear God, you take care of everything you have made. Thank you for sending rain to make the grass grow. Amen.”

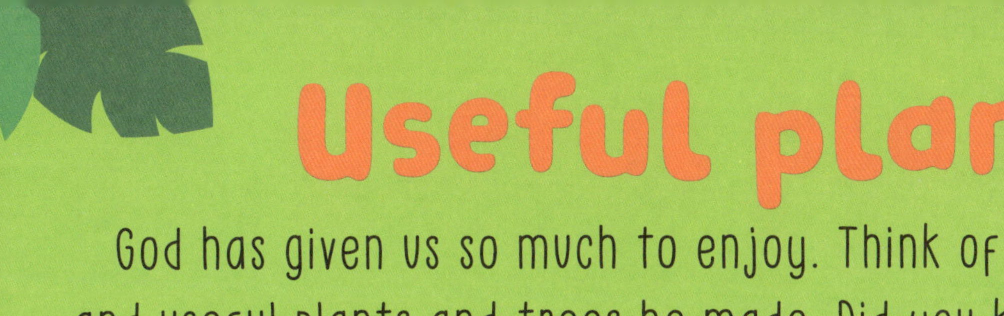

Useful plants

God has given us so much to enjoy. Think of all the beautiful and useful plants and trees he made. Did you know that we make chips, chocolate, and orange juice from plants and trees? Perfumes and medicines come from plants too. God must love us a lot to give us all these good things!

“Dear God, You made a beautiful world with so many good things. Thank You for giving us so much. Amen.”

Psalm 104:1–14 is a thank-you song to God for making a world full of good things.

"I want it!"

Katie knows she shouldn't take something without asking, but she wanted her friend's toy so much that she snatched it. Now she's been scolded. When we're upset because we can't have what we want, we can talk to God. He understands and will help us.

"Dear God, thank you for my toys. Help me not to take toys away from others. Amen."

Jesus has given us rules about how to live happily together. See Matthew 7:12.

"I'm angry!"

Do you get angry sometimes? When we get angry, we can say or do awful things, and that makes God sad. God wants us to talk to him when we're angry. We can tell him exactly how we feel. He always understands, and he can help us to be patient and kind like him.

Find out what God is like in Psalm 86:15.

**"Dear God,
I'm sorry I do bad things when I'm angry. Please help me to be like you. Amen."**

Going home

It's home time! Now that Arwen is at school, she has to put her coat on by herself. Then she runs outside to show her mom what she's made at school. It's lovely to go home after a busy day. Who comes to pick you up from school? Do you chat about your day just like Arwen?

The young man in this story is very glad to be home again. See Luke 15:11–24.

“Dear God, I'm glad I don't go home alone. Thank you for

....

who is there to fetch me. Amen.”

Snowflakes

Have you ever caught a snowflake? Each one is beautiful. Every snowflake has its own pattern and is different from all the others. Isn't that amazing? When lots of snowflakes fall at once, it makes a pretty white blanket over everything. What a wonderful world God has created!

"God in heaven, everything you have made is good. Even snowflakes show how wonderful you are. Amen."

God makes the weather – the ice, the frost, and the snow. See Psalm 147:15–18.

Making friends

It's fun making friends. We meet new friends in all sorts of places – at school, at church, and at playgroups. Where did you meet your friends? Tara's family has just moved to the town where Joe lives. Tara is a bit shy, but she's being brave and talking to Joe. They both love to play house!

When Paul moved to a new town, who made friends with him? See Acts 16:11–15.

“Dear God, I like my friends. Please help me to be friendly to new people, and please help me when I feel shy. Amen.”

Talking

Do you like talking? It's fun to tell our friends about all the exciting things we've done, and it's good to share sad times too. If something amazing has happened, who do you tell first? Do you tell your friends about the amazing things God does? Can you think of something you could tell them this week?

In Luke 8:38–39, Jesus helps a man and tells him to talk to the whole town about it!

"Dear God, help me to tell my friends how much you love them. Amen."

Building

Zoey and Alex have had fun making a fort under the table. On rainy days, they make a fort inside. On sunny days, they make a fort outside. They love making forts together. Isn't it great that God gives us friends? Who makes forts with you?

Paul liked making tents. In Acts 18:1–3, he met some friends who also made tents. Who were they?

"Making things is great fun, God! Thank you for my friend, ... We have fun together. Amen."

Your body

God has given us wonderful bodies. Let's see what yours can do!
Can you crouch down on the ground? Can you twirl around?
Can you stretch up really high? Can you blink or close one eye?
Can you hop, jump, or clap? If you can, thank God for that!

"Thank you, dear God, for my body and for all the amazing things I can do with it! Amen."

Psalm 139:13–14 tells us that God created every part of us.

Day and night

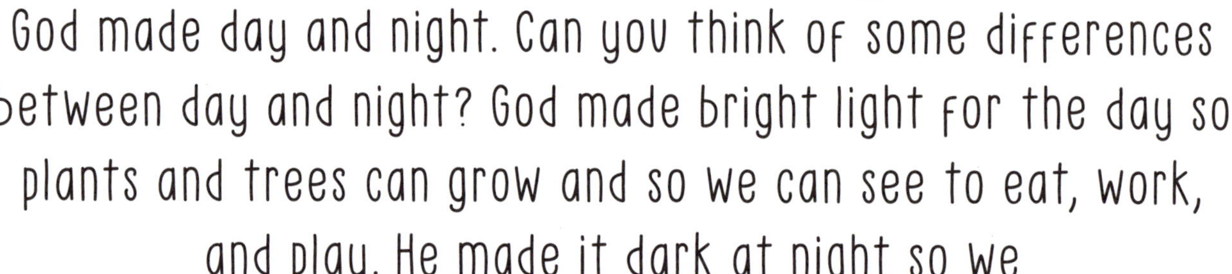

God made day and night. Can you think of some differences between day and night? God made bright light for the day so plants and trees can grow and so we can see to eat, work, and play. He made it dark at night so we can rest and sleep.

"Dear God, you made the day and the sun so bright. You made the moon and the dark, dark night! Amen."

Find out what God thought about making light. Read Genesis 1:3–5.

Counting stars

Can you count the stars in the sky? When God made the universe, he filled it with millions of stars. Did you know that there are more stars than there are grains of sand on all the beaches of the world? How awesome of God to make such an enormous universe for all those stars!

God tells Abraham to go out and count the stars. Find out what happens in Genesis 15:5–6.

“God, you're really great at imagining and making things. I love all the stars you made! Amen.”

Bath and bubbles

It's bath time! Daniel and Ollie love baths. Daniel likes to play with his toys, and Ollie loves splashing around. They both wash all over too! What do you do in the bathtub? Do you like to have lots of bubbles in your bath or none at all?

Peter once asked Jesus to give him a bath! Find out why in John 13:2–17.

“Dear God, thank you for warm water. At bath time, I like to .... Amen.”

Afraid of the dark

Joely is very tired, but she doesn't want to go to sleep because she's scared of the dark. Whenever we're afraid, we can ask God to care for us. He has promised to protect us. God is more powerful than anything, and he's not afraid of the dark!

God has promised to take care of you. Read Psalm 91:1–6.

"Dear God, when I'm scared or can't get to sleep, help me to remember that you're always there for me. Amen."

101

"Goodnight, God!"

It's time for stories, time for songs, time for hugs, and time for bed! Snuggle under your covers, shut your eyes, and think of all the fun things you did today. It's time to say a goodnight prayer and thank God for everything.

You can talk to God wherever you are, even lying in your bed! See Psalm 63:6–7.

"I'm snuggled up in bed, thoughts are running through my head. Thank you, God, for my busy day. Keep me close to you, I pray. Amen."

Themed contents

Your feelings

Your world

Your family

Relationships

Your body

God's creation

Christian Life